The Cruthin Controversy

Michael Hall

ISLAND 7 PAMPHLETS

Published 1994 by Island Publications
132 Serpentine Road, Newtownabbey, Co Antrim BT36 7JQ

© Michael Hall

ISBN 0 9514194 8 X

Printed by Regency Press, Belfast

The Cruthin

Our Predominant Ancestors
The first settlers arrived in Ireland around 6500 BC during the Mesolithic Age, archaeological evidence suggesting that they came from Galloway in south-west Scotland or Cumbria in northern England. [1] These first settlers were hunter-gatherers, but after 4000 BC, during the Neolithic Age, farming was introduced and man began clearing the thickly wooded Irish countryside. The Neolithic Irish also erected numerous stone burial monuments, surviving examples of which still retain the power to inspire and impress with their enigmatic grandeur.

Some of these structures reveal a close 'Scottish connection' – one type, the *court cairn*, is found in the north of Ireland and south-west Scotland, a fact which led Seán O Ríordáin to conclude: "The tombs and the finds from them form a continuous province joined rather than divided by the narrow waters of the North Channel." [2]

These Neolithic inhabitants of Ireland, far from being an obscure people lost in the mists of our distant past, were, in reality, the *predominant* ancestors of the Irish people of today. As archaeologist Peter Woodman explained:

> The gene pool of the Irish was probably set by the end of the Stone Age when there were very substantial numbers of people present and the landscape had already been frequently altered. The Irish are essentially Pre-Indo-European, they are not physically Celtic. No invasion since could have been sufficiently large to alter that fact completely. [3]

This fact must seem greatly at odds with the popular belief that the Irish are a predominantly *Celtic* people, yet scholars have increasingly come to accept that when the Celts arrived in Ireland they probably did so in numbers "far inferior to the native population(s)." [4]

The 'Isles of the Pretani'
Around 330 BC the Greek geographer and voyager, Pytheas, gave us the earliest reference to the British Isles, calling them the 'Isles of the Pretani', the *Pretani* thus becoming the oldest inhabitants of Britain and Ireland to whom a definite name has been given.

Were these Pretani part of the incoming Celtic minority, or part of the *pre*-Celtic population? If the latter, it is possible they were direct descendants of the Neolithic Irish, for up until the Celtic intrusions there is no evidence of any major immigrations into Ireland after the Neolithic period. Eoin MacNeill, co-founder of the Gaelic League, believed them to be pre-Celtic. In *Saorstát Eireann Official Handbook* he wrote:

> While the Celts were still newcomers to Ireland and Britain, the inhabitants of both countries were known to them by the name Pretani or Qreteni. From Qreteni came their old name in Irish – Cruithin... Later on, before A.D. 300, a new name, Scotti, began to be used in Latin for the people of Ireland, and a new name, Picti, for the people formerly called Pretani, then inhabiting the northern parts of Britain...
>
> Irish traditions amply confirm the evidence of Greek writers that Ireland was once a country of the Pretani, Cruithin, or Picts. Our own writers, in the seventh century and later, show that in their time there were numerous families, including many of high degree, in every quarter of Ireland but especially in Ulster and Connacht, who were recognised to be of Pictish descent. The problem 'Who were the Picts?' has long been under discussion. Ancient and firm tradition, in Britain as well as Ireland, declared them to be quite a distinct people from the Gaels and the Britons; and some who have sought to solve the problem have ignored the existence of a large Pictish element in Ireland. The view of the late Sir John Rhys appears most reasonable, that, whereas the Celts came from Mid-Europe and belonged to the 'Indo-European' linguistic group, the Picts belong to the older peoples of Western Europe. [5]

Although some of the views held by historians such as MacNeill are now deemed to be "out of fashion with many modern scholars"[6], his depiction of the Cruthin differs little from that presented by eminent scholars today. In a contribution to a modern text book on Irish history, Francis Byrne wrote:

> The earlier, non-Indo-European, population, of course, survived under the Celtic overlordship. One group in particular, known to the P-Celts as *Pritani* and to the Irish as *Cruithni*, survived into historical times as the Picts or 'painted people' of Scotland. The Cruithni were numerous in Ulster too, and the Loíges of Leinster and possibly the Ciarraige of Connacht and north Kerry belonged to the same people. [7]

Alongside this assertion that the Cruthin were pre-Celtic, is the suggestion that they shared an affinity with the Picts of Scotland. Although such a suggestion is contested by some academics today, it was one frequently made by the ancient Irish themselves, as Ian Adamson has summarised:

> ...when medieval Irish writers referred to [the Cruthin] it is clear they considered them to inhabit both Ireland and Scotland. One writer stated that 'thirty kings of the Cruthin ruled Ireland and Scotland from Ollam to Fiachna mac Baetáin,' and that 'seven kings of the Cruthin of Scotland ruled Ireland in Tara ' (*secht ríg do Chruithnibh Alban rofhallnastair Erind i Temair*) – thereby identifying, as T F O'Rahilly notes, "the Cruthin of Ireland with those of Scotland." Others refer to Scotland as the 'land of the Cruthin', while in a poem written in the eleventh or twelfth century the

author tells us that the *Cruthnig* made up a section of the population of Scotland. The Annals of Tigernach, The Pictish Chronicle, St Berchan, the Albanic Duan, the Book of Deer and John of Fordun plainly show that the name Cruthin was applied to the inhabitants of both Scotland and Ireland. [8(E)]

Academics who discount any link between the Irish Cruthin and the Scottish Picts often point out that while ancient texts written in Irish may have used the label 'Cruthin' to signify both peoples, texts written in Latin never used the word 'Picts' for the Irish Cruthin. However, this could be a product of the efforts by ancient Gaelic genealogists not only to disassociate the Irish Cruthin from the Scottish Picts, but to dispense with the name 'Cruthin' itself, and provide the Cruthin with a Gaelic ancestry instead. As T F O'Rahilly explained:

> The combined influence of Bede, Mael Mura, and the genealogical fiction of Ir, caused *Cruithni* to lose favour as the name of a section of the Irish population. This disuse of *Cruithni* as a name is doubtless connected with the rise of a new genealogical doctrine which turned the Irish Cruthin into Gaels and thus disassociated them from the Cruthin of Scotland. Nevertheless the fact that there were Cruthin in Ireland as well as in Scotland was, as might be expected, long remembered; and so it is not surprising to find writers occasionally suggesting, in defiance of Mael Mura, that the Cruthin of both countries formed one people in remote times. [9]

While there is no actual 'proof' of any ethnic affinity between sections of the population in Ireland and Scotland, circumstantially there is much that would make it a strong possibility: the close proximity of the two areas; the archaeological evidence of contact dating back to the Stone Age; the fact that population movements across the North Channel have been a *constant* feature throughout history; and the belief held by some scholars that both the Irish Cruthin[7] and the Scottish Picts[10] were pre-Celtic peoples.

As Liam de Paor concluded:

> The gene pool of the Irish... is probably very closely related to the gene pools of highland Britain.... With that fringe area, relationships, both cultural and genetic, almost certainly go back to a much more distant time than that uncertain period when Celtic languages and customs came to dominate both Great Britain and Ireland. Therefore, so far as the physical make-up of the Irish goes... they share these origins with their fellows in the neighbouring parts – the north and west – of the next-door island of Great Britain. [11]

Struggle for Dominance

Despite the Celts being a minority within the population, they began to wield an enormous amount of influence and power. Whatever the reasons for this – military prowess, superior weapons, tactical skills, or even the dynastic way they parcelled out their conquests – they gradually came to dominate large areas of the island, aided by alliances forged with sections of the indigenous people.

That the Cruthin continued to play an important role in Irish political and military affairs is well documented in ancient texts, especially with regard to the constant struggle for control of Ulster. The attempts by one of the most dynamic of the Celtic dynasties, the Gaelic Uí Néill, to dominate the North – opposed fiercely by the Cruthin in alliance with the Celtic Ulaid – is evidenced by the numerous battles listed in the ancient annals.

For example, in 563 AD at the battle of Móin Dairi Lothair (Moneymore) seven Cruthin kings were slain, the compiler of the *Annals of Ulster* also recording the event in verse:

> Sharp weapons stretch, men stretch,
> In the great bog of Daire-lothair –
> The cause of a contention for right –
> Seven Cruithnian Kings, including Aedh Brec.
> The battle of all the Cruithni is fought
> [And] they burn Eilne.
> The battle of Gabhair-Lifè is fought,
> And the battle of Cul-dreimne. [12]

Another battle is recorded between the Cruthin and the Uí Néill near Coleraine in 579, and in 637 occurred the mightiest clash of all – the battle of Moira, described by Sir Samuel Ferguson as the "greatest battle, whether we regard the numbers engaged, the duration of combat, or the stake at issue, ever fought within the bounds of Ireland." [13] The Ulstermen on that occasion were led by the Cruthin over-king of Ulster, Congal Cláen. No doubt the Ulstermen were hoping to undo some of the Uí Néill gains, and probably felt they had good prospects of doing so, especially when, as Francis Byrne pointed out,

> ...we remember that the Ulaid and Cruthin were still powerful in County Londonderry and possibly still ruled directly in Louth as far as the Boyne in the early seventh century; that they cherished memories of their former dominance over all the North; that they considered the Uí Néill recent upstarts... [14]

In another confrontation at Leth Cam (near Armagh) in 827 the Uí Néill king, the Cruthin king, the Ulaid king and many princes of Ulster were killed. By this time the label 'Cruthin' had been superseded by the names of individual septs, and the main body of Cruthin were known as the Dál nAraidi.

Ironically it was not until 1364, after the Gaelic chiefs had destroyed the first Anglo-Normans to set foot in the North, that a Uí Néill chief could at last style himself 'king of Ulster'.

Europe's Debt to Bangor

Not all the Cruthin owe their fame to positions of kingship or deeds on the battlefield. In 555 AD St Comgall, perhaps the most illustrious of all the Cruthin, founded a monastic school at Bangor (County Down), which was to achieve great historic importance.

Such was his reputation for piety and learning that multitudes flocked to his school from the most distant parts; it is well established that not less than 3,000 students and teachers were under his care at one time, including many of the most honourable in the land. The evangelistic zeal of Comgall was pre-eminent – down to the landing-place at the reef of rocks he led many a band of his disciples who were to embark on their frail coracles to spread the Gospel in European countries. [15]

An early text – Adamnan's *Life of Columba* – not only depicts a meeting between Comgall and another famous religious personality, St Columba, the latter a prince of the Uí Néill, but gives a clear indication that the Cruthin were still perceived as having a distinct identity:

At another time [Columba] and the abbot Comgall sit down not far from the fortress [of Cethirn], on a bright summer's day. Then water is brought to the Saints in a brazen vessel from a spring hard by, for them to wash their hands. Which when St Columba had received, he thus speaks to the abbot Comgall, who is sitting beside him: 'The day will come, O Comgall, when that spring, from which has come the water now brought to us, will not be fit for any human purposes.' 'By what cause,' says Comgall, 'will its spring water be corrupted?' Then says St Columba, 'Because it will be filled with human blood, for my family friends and thy relations according to the flesh, that is, the Uí Néill and the Cruthin people, will wage war, fighting in this fortress of Cethirn close by. Whence in the above-named spring some poor fellow of my kindred will be slain, and the basin of the same spring will be filled with the blood of him that is slain with the rest.' Which true prophecy of his was fulfilled in its season after many years. [16]

One of Comgall's disciples was Columbanus, who in 589 set off on a great missionary journey through Europe, eventually dying at Bobbio, Italy. The monasteries he established throughout his travels were the inspiration for hundreds of others. Robert Schuman, the French Foreign Minister whose energies contributed greatly to the setting up of the European Economic Community, said that "St. Columbanus is the patron saint of those who seek to construct a united Europe".

An Important Legacy?
The Cruthin, therefore, hold a prominent position in our history:

- They are the first people in Ireland to whom a definite name can be attached.

- It is accepted that they once comprised the majority of the population in large areas of Ulster.

- They were to the forefront in the interminable warfare which took place during Ulster's early history.

- They produced several important historical personages, one of whom was to have a lasting impact not only upon Irish but upon European history.

- The Cruthin were among those settlers from Ulster, labelled 'Scotti' by the Romans, who migrated across the North Channel and gave 'Scotland' its name. Their descendants in turn were undoubtedly among those Scots who came to Ulster during the 17th century Plantation. They are an integral part of the multi-faceted 'connection' between the peoples of Scotland and Ireland, which, when properly explored, might help to unify the presently-divided communities in Ulster, and even 'bridge the gap' between the peoples of our two islands. [This theme is explored in greater depth in my other pamphlets *Ulster's Scottish Connection,*[17] and *Ulster's Shared Heritage.*[18]]

An impressive pedigree, it would seem, and one which surely must have accorded the Cruthin a prominent place in our historical heritage. And yet the excellent Ulster Museum makes no mention of them, nor the exciting new visitor's centre at Navan Fort, possibly Ulster's most important antiquity. And, until recently, many books on Irish history paid them scant attention, if not ignoring them completely.

It is Dr Ian Adamson who has been primarily responsible for bringing this 'forgotten' aspect of our heritage to the attention of the general public. Yet the work of Adamson and myself is deemed to be so much at variance with both 'received' and 'popular' opinion, we are often accused of 'making it all up'. A review of my *Ulster: The Hidden History* [19] said that it was "naive [and aimed] at nothing less than an overthrow of current perceptions",[20] while Adamson's work has attracted a litany of derogatory comments: "a house of cards – half-truths and fanciful suppositions built one upon another"[21] . . . "spurious authenticity"[22] . . . "concocted"[21] . . . "disputed theories"[23] . . ."sheer disbelief from leading academics"[24]. . . "academically eccentric"[25] . . . and many more in the same vein.

The matter has engendered surprising emotions from among a profession usually thought of as being somewhat sedate and aloof. One prominent academic, while in a mini-bus with other academics, launched into a tirade against Adamson that was 'hysterical' rather than 'historical', during which he informed his astonished colleagues that if any of them owned copies of Adamson's books "they should go home and burn them all!"

'Advisors' to the Northern Ireland Office have apparently informed officials there that the 'Cruthin theory' is either 'eccentric' or a form of Loyalist extremism.

One local author almost published a ludicrous falsehood about my own book which she said had been relayed to her by 'reliable sources', without either this author or her 'source' having felt any need to check the facts with me.

Who are these 'advisors' and what expertise do they claim; *what* is the real basis to the intense academic antagonism; and *why* do 'reliable sources' feel the necessity to deal in falsehoods? To help explore such questions, the second part of this pamphlet will be an analysis of the controversy which has surrounded 'Cruthinism', as one writer[22] labelled it, for this controversy has become as fascinating a 'story' as that of the Cruthin themselves.

The Controversy

'Revisionism' or 'Rediscovery'?

When Ian Adamson first wrote about the Cruthin, it was obvious that his subject matter was totally unknown to the general public. Popular awareness of Ireland's past was a collage of themes, personalities and dates – the Celts, St Patrick, the Vikings, Gaelic chiefs and English conquerors, Plantation and Rebellion, William and James, 1690 and the Boyne, 1916 and the Easter Rising or the Somme, Independence and Partition... but no Cruthin. Even to those with a knowledge of, or training in, Irish history, Adamson's thesis appeared to be so out of step with accepted thinking that it was deemed either a complete fabrication, or a skilful attempt to 'rewrite' our past. Graduates in History from Queen's University, Belfast, dismissed our work as "pure revisionism", while lecturers wrote of "the revisionism inherent in the Cruthin thesis". [26] Now, a charge of 'revisionism' is usually engendered by a belief that the thesis being presented is simply an attempt to 'remould' history to make it conform to a 'new' perspective. But *was* what we were revealing really all that 'new' or even 'revised'?

In the first part of this pamphlet I quoted from Eoin MacNeill's contribution to *Saorstát Eireann Official Handbook*, which was published in 1932. I could cite similar examples from the same period. Indeed, it is possible to go back even further, over 100 years in fact, to the ninth edition of the *Encyclopaedia Britannica*, [27] which not only makes clear reference to the Cruthin but speaks of their ethnic affinity with the Scottish Picts. The Cruthin, therefore, were never 'concocted' by Adamson; on the contrary, the numerous references to them by other scholars provides, as W A Hanna pointed out,

> ...indisputable evidence that Adamson did not conjure up the Cruthin as an early pre-Celtic people in Ireland, that he was not the first to suggest that some of them emigrated from Ulster to Scotland, and that he did not invent the theory of their return. [6]

However, between the period during which those earlier references were written, throughout the traumatic birth of modern Ireland and up until quite recently, things *had* changed. Mention of the Cruthin had disappeared from many history books (including the edition of the *Encyclopaedia Britannica* currently held in Belfast Central Library) – a *revision*. Mention even of a significant pre-Celtic population inhabiting Ireland alongside the Celts was ignored, the majority of the Irish people were now apparently all Celts – a *revision*. Any suggestion of an ethnic affinity between the ancient inhabitants of Scotland and Ulster was sidelined – a *revision*. 'Revisionism' had indeed been undertaken, *not* by Adamson, but by sections of the academic elite. Adamson had simply endeavoured to bring this 'hidden' aspect of our shared heritage to the attention of our divided community.

Some might contend that even if Adamson and I have not 'revised' history as such, we are simply resurrecting notions about our past which have long since been abandoned. That this is patently not the case should become clear in the exploration which follows.

Academic Distaste for 'Popular Historians'

1989 saw the publication of a new history of Ulster written by leading academics. According to the editors the volume had its origins in "a demand from both teachers of history and the general public for an accessible and up-to-date history of the province. Though recent years have seen the publication of a number of scholarly monographs dealing with aspects of Ulster's past, *the last general history of the province was published in the 1950s.*"[28] [my italics]

According to the editors, then, a great vacuum in books on Ulster's history aimed at a general audience has seemingly existed for decades. No acknowledgement here of Adamson's *The Cruthin*, or *The Identity of Ulster*, or my own *Ulster: The Hidden History*, even though two of these titles were specifically 'general histories of the province', and all of them went into reprint(s) and, in local terms at least, became best sellers (and all of them far more 'accessible' to the 'general public' than the academic volume with its £18 cover price). The truth is that the editors *were* well aware of these books, and also that the "demand from the general public" *was* being met – the problem was that this was originating not from within academia, but from among – using the description of one of their contributors – 'popular historians', which in rough translation means 'non-professionals'.

Richard Warner, from the Department of Antiquities at the Ulster Museum, acknowledged the root of the problem when he admonished his fellow scholars: "It is an absolute obligation on professionals to make [their interpretations of] history available to everybody else so that they can absorb it and assimilate it as part of their history. If the professionals fail to do that then they have only themselves to blame when the non-professionals take up the history wrongly."[29]

The 'professionals' had indeed been ignoring Adamson. As Peter Carr pointed out: "Liberal academia... kept its distance. Adamson after all was distinctly non-U, an outsider, a prole, a mere BA." [20] Academia would have preferred that the vacuum had been filled by themselves: to them Adamson was indeed an 'outsider' and the writing of history is best left in the hands of 'professionals'. As Richard Warner unabashedly asserted on behalf of his fellow academics: "Well, I hate to sound arrogant, but [it is] the job of people like me to know when history is likely to be correct or historical interpretation is likely to be correct or incorrect." [29]

Well, to be honest, it *does* sounds arrogant, but we could live with that – if it was simply a matter of academic sensitivities and professional/non-professional jealousies. The problem is that academia has had plenty of opportunities to fill the vacuum, but, for whatever reasons, has not only 'kept its distance' from Adamson, but has kept its distance from the communal tragedy which has been going on with unabated intensity outside its ivory towers.

One academic admitted this to us privately: "For twenty years now our two communities have been murdering each other, supposedly *over their history*, and what have our academics done about it? Absolutely nothing! They've washed their hands of any responsibility, content to collect their salaries, their bursaries, their grants... just sat on their backsides and observed events with an aloof cynicism, without the slightest suggestion that *they* could play any role confronting it. The general public has received more 'history lessons' from gable-wall muralists than from the whole of academia."

Academic Dilemma

That academics hoped that 'Cruthinism' might 'go away' was pointed out by Brian Lambkin: "The initial reception of *The Cruthin* by the community of scholars in early Irish history did little to alleviate the sense of exclusion. It was largely ignored. Understandably, scholars felt themselves faced with a dilemma: to engage with the debate opened up by Adamson would be to give it a spurious authenticity..." [22]

I would contend that, contrary to a supposed concern with 'spurious authenticity', academia was more troubled that an outsider had caught them so unprepared. They knew that much of the history Adamson was dealing with *was* 'authentic' – even if they quarrelled with his particular interpretations – the problem was that having someone outside the 'club' reveal it was a poor reflection on themselves and their outdated fixations. Academic vested interests were now under the spotlight, and for some it was an unaccustomed experience, as one reviewer witnessed:

> I remember, several years ago, listening with astonishment to a leading archaeologist telling a persistent questioner at a public lecture, in suitably polite and academic language, to think what he was told to think. The questioner's fatal error had been to raise the subject of the Cruthin. [30]

When Adamson in his most recent books began to substantiate his analysis by numerous quotes from eminent academics it drew an astonishing rebuke: "...it would be easier to accept his overall thesis if it were less dependent on selective extracts from other historians." [31] I suspect that this aversion to the use of such 'extracts' had little to do with 'acceptance', but reflected the discomfiture felt within sections of academia at the sight of an array of quotes apparently lending credence to Adamson's thesis. Better to keep Adamson at a distance, an eccentric "pseudo-historian" [21], that have him appear to be expounding theories for which he could produce scholarly support; for, as W A Hanna pointed out, his "references... clearly show that far from 'concocting' anything Adamson has merely restated the views of others, mostly highly respected and reputable historians." [6]

Into the Fray...
Once it became clear that 'Cruthinism' could not be ignored, it attracted an assortment of reviewers and critics into battle against it. Sometimes their motive was less than clear; indeed, some openly admitted it was an area of history they knew little about – "I am not qualified to gauge the factual basis of Adamson's thesis" [31], or "I am not in a position to quarrel with the historical accuracy of this account..." [32] – yet this did not stop them from launching into their critiques. It was almost as if 'anyone who was anybody' in intellectual circles felt a need to have said something about the subject, perhaps even to have said it with flair and panache: "somewhere in the heaven of lost reviews hovers the one I should have liked to have written." [31]

'Confronting the issue...'
While reviewers and assorted armchair critics dabbled in the 'controversy' almost from its first appearance, mainstream academia was more reluctant to become involved in any frontal attack, preferring to snipe occasionally from the sidelines. Indeed, as Brian Lambkin pointed out: "It took until 1989... for an established scholar to confront the issue in a popular book and demonstrate the flaws in Adamson's hypothesis." [22] Lambkin's reference is to a contribution by Charles Doherty in *Ulster: An Illustrated History*, the academic volume already referred to, though whether any flaws were indeed 'demonstrated' is highly debatable.

Doherty begins by pointing out that: "Some popular historians have claimed that the Cruthin were the original [pre-Gaelic] population group to occupy the north-east... who held out against Gaelic 'invaders'...." He disputes this 'interpretation', saying that "much of this theory is derived from the work of the late T F O'Rahilly whose historical conclusions have been questioned by archaeologists and historians. In particular, O'Rahilly's thesis on the chronology of the invasion has been subject to serious revision and, consequently... his views on the ethnic makeup of early Ireland are no longer accepted." [33]

Doherty seems to be trying to negate 'Cruthinism' by making it appear dependent upon O'Rahilly's disputed ethnic analysis. However, Adamson found O'Rahilly's work invaluable *not* because of the latter's views on the 'ethnic makeup' of the Irish, but because of his astute analysis as to how the ancient Irish historians had submerged the distinctive identity of the Cruthin.

Doherty himself endeavours to blur any such distinctions among the ancient Irish: "...it is dangerous to assign racial origins to any particular tribal group in early Ireland. Such was the degree of homogenization of the various peoples of prehistoric Ireland that by the opening of the historical period they had all gone 'native'..." [33]

Ironically, despite the attempts to downgrade any distinctive Cruthin identity, academics can easily reverse the process when it suits and suddenly rediscover such 'distinctions' and 'differences'. For example, when Richard Warner wished to counter the suggestion that the people in control of Emain Macha (Navan) were all Cruthin (something which was never claimed by Adamson), he was quite adamant in his response:

> The Ulaid became the tribe in historic times living in County Down called the Dál Fiatach, and all the historians of that time made a *clear distinction* between [them] and the Dál nAraidi of County Antrim who were Cruthin. It was *absolutely clear* that the Dál Fiatach of County Down and the Ulaid of Navan *were Érainn*. They belonged to *exactly the same ethnic* grouping as the people in the south, who [according to the early myths] they were apparently fighting. *The fact is* that the people in Navan... and the Cruthin were *totally different.* [29] [my italics]

Although Doherty goes on to talk of the Cruthin as if he had no dispute with Adamson (he says they "formed the bulk of the population in the reduced over-kingdom of the Ulaid", that their name "implies an ancient population group", and he even makes mention of their "most powerful king", Congal), it is evident his main disagreement with Adamson is whether the Cruthin can be labelled pre-Gaelic. As he explained on a radio programme:

> ...if there was some memory of the Cruthin as being pre-Goidelic or pre-Celtic or whatever, there is no way of getting at it now from the sources and those who would try to use it that way I think are really picking and choosing material that suit their thesis and not examining the evidence on its own part. [29]

He is suggesting that the most logical assumption – going by 'the evidence' – is that the Cruthin were *not* pre-Celtic, and that to see them otherwise requires a deliberate manipulation of this 'evidence'. *Surely the opposite is the case* – that it is *far more likely* that the Cruthin *were* pre-Celtic, and it is those wishing to see them as *Celts* who have to do the 'picking and choosing'. The supposed 'Celticity' of the Irish has come under such increasing attack within academia that even Doherty is forced to tread more circumspectly: "It is likely that the distant ancestors of [the Cruthin] may even have been pre-Celtic." [33]

Suggesting that the 'distant' ancestors *may* have been pre-Celts, implies that the 'immediate' ancestors *were* Celts. But if, as most scholars now accept, 'the evidence' suggests that the Celts were only a small minority in Ireland, who then were these *Celtic Cruthin* – especially if the Cruthin, far from being a minority, composed, as Doherty himself admitted, "the bulk of the population group in the reduced over-kingdom of the Ulaid"? How is it possible for the Celts be a 'small minority' *and* 'the bulk of the population' *at the same time?* Academics repeatedly assert that Adamson is confused as to who the Cruthin *were* – we could equally contend that academics are just as confused as to who they *were not*.

Adamson and myself have actually *no problem* accepting that Irish society became thoroughly 'homogenized'; our contention has always been that the Irish were basically a pre-Celtic people, to whom a Celtic minority made a significant political and cultural contribution. Indeed, we would readily agree with Richard Warner that:

> Throughout [some 700 years of the Early Iron Age] the mass of the Irish people remained racially unchanged. Whatever they were at the end of the Bronze age they were still, with a small but important addition (partly at least from the Celtic world), when they entered the early medieval period. [34]

Rather than *our* analysis – that this 'unchanging mass' was pre-Celtic – being under threat, we feel it is the attempt by Doherty and others to 'distance' the bulk of the Irish from their pre-Celtic inheritance which should prove the more difficult assertion to sustain.

"Hardly Discussable"?

Adamson's theories as to the origins of the Cruthin have been dismissed by some archaeologists as "hardly discussable since the Cruthin as a distinct ethnic group are archaeologically invisible, that is, there is not a single object or site that an archaeologist can declare to be distinctly Cruthin." [35]

This is surprising logic, to say the least. The Cruthin had a definite name for themselves; are referred to repeatedly in the ancient Irish annals; are clearly identified in Adamnan's *Life of Columba*; are mentioned in that great saga of the Ulster Cycle, the *Táin*; and it is widely accepted that they formed the bulk of the population over a sizeable part of Ulster – yet because they are "archaeologically invisible" theories about them, it appears, are "hardly discussable"? This seems especially ironic when we consider that, apart from the legacy of their language, there is no real evidence as to when the *Celts* arrived in Ireland, no real idea as to their numbers other than the probability that they only constituted a small minority, and when even the notion that the Irish could be called 'Celts' only originated in the 19th century (the ancient Irish never thought of themselves as Celts) – yet for years academics have not only felt perfectly able to 'discuss' the Celts at great length but have developed a minor industry writing books about them.

Archaeologists Mallory and McNeill concluded that: "when the Cruthin of Ulster emerge in our earliest texts they bear Irish names and there is not the slightest hint that they spoke anything other than Irish." [35] 'Not the slightest hint'? Surely it is not as clear-cut as that. When Columba went to convert the Scottish Picts he is said to have been accompanied by the Cruthin abbot of Bangor, Comgall, whose possible role – according to some scholars – was to act as 'interpreter'. And, as Richard Warner cautioned: "We should take heed of O'Rahilly's claim that as late as the sixth century 'Irish' (that is, the language we call Irish) was not the only language spoken in Ireland." [34]

Brickbats over the 'Wall'

When Adamson's book *The Ulster People* was published, and featured in a *Belfast Telegraph* article, Richard Warner wrote to the newspaper[36] with a refutation of comments made about the series of ancient linear earthworks collectively known as the 'Black Pig's Dyke', still visible at various places along Ulster's southern boundary.

Warner attempted to take Adamson to task for speculating about matters for which he insisted "there is no evidence". One must assume that Warner is opposed to all such speculation. Yet, a glaring inconsistency exists. Warner is a member of the Navan Research Group who publish the academic journal *Emania*. One issue contained the results of an investigation into a section of the Dyke by Aidan Walsh, Curator of Monaghan County Museum, which, according to the editor, provided "our first solid evidence for both the construction and dating of this monument". In the article, Walsh, as he is entitled to do, makes various speculations on the basis of his investigation. It is interesting to contrast some of these with Warner's forceful denunciation of those by Adamson.

Warner asserts that "there is no evidence that the various pieces of earthwork ever formed a continuous boundary", and that "there is no evidence that they were built at one time". There may indeed be no solid evidence, but Aidan Walsh felt confident enough after *his* survey to propose: "We can now begin to think of a frontier composed of various scattered earthworks and we can begin to suggest that they might be linked together in time and origin."[37]

Warner further states that "there is no evidence of a palisade on top". There may not have been a palisade *on top*, but Warner omitted to point out that there is, however, evidence of a palisade *adjoining* the Dyke. In the portion investigated by Walsh, a third line of defence was discovered which "was composed of a timber palisade which paralleled the earthwork itself... This palisade was sizeable [and] could have stood up to 3-4 metres in height." In a separate investigation Chris Lynn also uncovered evidence of a palisade at the 'Dorsey ramparts' further to the east.

Warner also asserts that "there is no evidence of a war between Ulster and the rest of the country in 100 BC". Yet Walsh felt able to speculate: "Perhaps we are dealing here with a series of extraordinary events in the centuries before Christ with a war extending across the land starting at the boundaries of a kingdom and culminating with the destruction of its capital."[37]

Warner may indeed heartily disagree with the speculations of his fellow academic; the interesting point is that he did not see fit – as far as I am aware – to dash to the local newspapers with a vigorous denunciation of Walsh's pronouncements. I suspect, therefore, that 'speculation' *per se* is not the problem – the problem for Warner, as it is for other academics, is Adamson and his Cruthin.

There is one final aspect to Warner's letter which merits comment. He states that the "general thesis of the book... is that archaeology proves that Ulster had a separateness in ancient times that is, somehow, relevant to the politics of today." Yet, not only is it patently *not* the "general thesis", but discussion of archaeology only takes up an extremely small part of the book. I suggest that readers of Adamson's book bear in mind Warner's assertion that it is "the job of people like me to know when... historical interpretation is likely to be correct or incorrect," [29] and judge for themselves whether his 'interpretation' of *The Ulster People* is 'correct or incorrect'.

'Deceptions of scholars'
The September 1993 edition of *Fortnight* magazine carried an article entitled 'Deception of demons' which presented itself as an authoritative 'refutation' of Adamson's theories. Its author, H J Morgan, formerly of the Department of Irish Studies and currently co-editor of *History Ireland*, began his 'refutation' with a personal attack on Adamson: "Dr Ian Adamson is a hospital doctor, not a doctor of philosophy. He has therefore, no training as a scholar. He is a *pseudo-historian* who distorts history for propaganda purposes." [21] Apart from being extremely offensive language this is also a highly questionable piece of logic. Given that so many 'scholarly' disciplines have been greatly enriched by the work of laymen or those who had not necessarily come up 'through the ranks', I would imagine other academics were astonished by Morgan's assertion. Some were certainly not appreciative of his tone: one expressed regret at Morgan's use of "insinuation and innuendo", pointing out that "personal attacks seldom convince the discerning reader". [6]

However, leaving that aside, here is Morgan's gripe: "[Adamson's] theory is nonsense and Adamson has a brass neck in expounding it. It is not an argument based on ascertainable facts but is, rather, a house of cards – half truths and fanciful suppositions built one upon another. A number of points can easily demolish this tenuous thesis..." [21]

Although I was greatly intrigued, and eagerly anticipated a challenging read, I was to be extremely disappointed. Let me go through Morgan's points:

> First, the Ulaid who ruled Ulster at the time of the cattle raid [of Cooley – *The Táin*] were *not* the Cruthin. The latter were a subject people of the Ulaid. There is even a reference in *The Annals of Ulster*, under AD 668, of a battle between the Ulaid and the Cruthin at Belfast. [21]

This 'point' seems to suggest that Adamson was *not aware* that: (i) the Ulaid and the Cruthin were different groupings; (ii) the Ulaid were in a position of dominance over the Cruthin; and (iii) the two groupings had even fought together at present-day Belfast. I can best respond by quoting directly from Adamson's *The Ulster People* :

> The Ulaid, according to Francis Byrne, "most probably represented a warrior caste of La Tène Celts from Britain, wielding an overlordship over indigenous tribes." Among these 'indigenous tribes', who obviously still formed the majority of the population, the most important and the most

populous were the *Cruthin*. These pre-Celtic peoples shared in the over-kingship of Ulster, particular those Cruthin later known as the Dál nAraidi... though at times the strains within the alliance would lead to open warfare (it was a battle between the Cruthin and Ulaid, recorded in the *Annals of Ulster* as having been fought at the 'Fearsat' in 667 which gave Belfast its first mention in history).[8(E)]

Can Morgan not read? I am assuming he had the courtesy, indeed the professionalism, to read *The Ulster People*; after all it had been available for two years and it would be highly reprehensible for someone who sets such high store in "training as a scholar" to have ignored his adversary's current work, especially when his attack was aimed on such a personal level. Let us proceed to Morgan's next point:

> Second, it is highly unlikely that Cú Chulainn was one of the Cruthin because his lands were in Co Louth and Cooley, the home of the Brown Bull, is also in Co Louth.[21]

I cannot imagine that Morgan is suggesting here that Cúchulainn's lands were not part of ancient Ulster, for most historians accept that they were; I presume that what he means is that Co Louth was not considered *Cruthin territory*. However, not all scholars would agree with him on that. Eoin MacNeill wrote:

> ...when Ireland emerges into the full light of written history, we find the Picts a very powerful people in east Ulster, Cuailnge itself, the home of the Brown Bull, and the neighbouring plain of Muirtheimhne, Cú Chulainn's patrimony, being now Pictish territory.[38]

An ancient text also links the Conaille of Louth alongside the other main Cruthin septs to the legendary Ulster warrior, Conall Cernach: " 'The clans of Conall *cernach*' are the Dalaradians, the *úi Echach ulad*, the *Conaille* of Murthemny, and 'the seven Soghans'." (L.L. 331:3)

Admittedly, uncertainty does exist, Byrne pointing out that there was disagreement among the genealogists as to the actual ethnic origins of the Conaille.[14] Yet although they were firmly linked to Ulster, it is doubtful that they were of the Ulaid, for the annals record repeated attacks upon them by the latter, and after Matudan of the Ulaid plundered the Conaille in 949 he was slain by the Conaille's immediate neighbours, the Cruthin of Iveagh. Was this just coincidence, or were the Iveagh Cruthin avenging an attack on their own?

However, even if we cannot say with certainty that the Conaille of Louth were Cruthin, what about Cúchulainn himself – or, more correctly, his legend? The ancient Irish writers were always at pains to glorify the dominant Gaelic ruling class, yet, as R A S Macalister pointed out:

> Those whom the chronicler wishes to exalt are fair, with long flowing hair. Those who are abased, in positions or morals, are as a rule dark, with close-cropped or 'rough' hair. There is, however, one remarkable exception to all these rules. The great Ultonian champion, Cú Chulaind, is described as being very dark, and close-cropped.[39]

Eoin MacNeill also commented on this anomaly:

> Cú Chulainn, according to one tradition preserved by Dubhaltach, belonged to a non-Gaelic tribe called Tuath Tabhairn, and it will be remembered that he is once described as 'a small dark man'. 'Thou little elf!' his charioteer used to call him, to provoke him to do his utmost in the fight. [62]

So here we have a hero who is small and dark – quite unlike the tall blond Celtic heroes – who apparently is not a Gael, but yet is not of the Ulaid either: "The MS Harleian 5280 tells us categorically that Cú Chulaind was exempt from (the 'sickness' of the Ulstermen), *ar nar bó don Ulltaib do*, 'for he was not of the Ulaid'." [39]

Adamson's contention that there is circumstantial evidence linking the legend of Cúchulainn to the pre-Celtic population, as likely as not the Cruthin, is just as valid, indeed probably more so, than Morgan's bland assertion that such a link is "highly unlikely". As for Morgan pointing out to us that "Cooley... is also in Co Louth", what can I say, other than to award full marks for geography!

To continue with Morgan's 'refutation':

> The term 'Cruthin' is Gaelic for 'Briton', but the British tribe with whom Adamson most frequently conflates the Cruthin are the Picts. The problem with this claim is that the Picts lived in the eastern parts of Scotland, from Fifeshire up to the Orkneys, and none of their highly-distinctive standing stones or high crosses has ever been found in Ulster. [21]

Fellow scholar, Charles Doherty, was also emphatic that "there is no archaeological evidence to suggest a Pictish connection". [33] However, lack of archaeological 'evidence' is hardly the most conclusive of yardsticks, as Mallory and McNeill revealed with regard to a later episode in Ulster's 'Scottish connection':

> History records how towards the end of the 5th century AD Ulstermen began conquering and colonizing southwestern Scotland to form the kingdom of Dál Riata which spanned the northern region of the Irish Sea... despite the fact that we believe we know when all this took pace, there is really not a shred of archaeological evidence to prove that it did happen. [35]

Although academics would contend that there is "no archaeological evidence" to suggest a Pictish connection, and that the Cruthin are "archaeologically invisible", they themselves appear to have a remarkable ability to 'see' into the remote past. Richard Warner said of any possible population movement across the North Channel: "...we are talking about a movement of ordinary people and these ordinary people were *not* the people who were moving in ancient times. It was only the kings who were moving about in ancient times." [29]

Anyway, to return to Morgan's 'critique'. His final comment is that "rather than dabbling in pre-history... the easiest way to throw out Adamson's theory is to show that the 17th-century settlers were not the descendents of the Cruthin. One-third of the planters were lowland Scots; one-third was English. The other third was, in fact, Gaelic..."

Again I ask: can Morgan not read, or is he *deliberately* misrepresenting Adamson? Adamson *never* said that all the planters were descendents of the Cruthin, and has not only detailed the *mixed* background of the newcomers, but challenged the popular notion that the Planters were even all Protestants. He makes it clear that while "*many*" of the Planters, "particularly those who came from areas in Scotland which in previous centuries had been populated by immigrants from Ulster, may be justly considered as returning to the home of their ancestors"[8(E)], at the same time:

> ...there were also elements of Brittonic stock from Strathclyde, with smaller elements of Norse, 'Norman', Anglo-Saxon, Dalriadan and Pictish stock as well... Furthermore those 'English' settlers planted by the Puritan Lord Deputy Sir Arthur Chichester were mostly from Lancashire, Cheshire and Devon and thus basically of Brittonic stock. The third element consisted of Londoners, twelve Companies of whom were given most of the county of Coleraine, whose name they changed to Londonderry. Most of them did not find the area to their liking, and soon returned to London....[8(A)]
>
> Neither must it be assumed that all the settlers were Protestants, since there were Scottish Catholics as well, some of whom, such as the Hume family of Derry, were ultimately of English origin... M. Perceval-Maxwell has confirmed that... one of the most successful parts of the Scottish Plantation was led by Roman Catholics... The new Scots settlers differed from the English in language on two counts. Firstly there was a significant group who spoke Gaelic and it seems that Scottish Gaelic speakers were intelligible to the Irish at this period. [8(D)]

Need I proceed any further? After having the effrontery to begin his 'refutation' with personal abuse and the assertion that he could "easily demolish this tenuous thesis", it is astonishing that Morgan failed to do his research properly, and revealed himself unable to substantiate such a pretentious claim, even if he was, as he himself admitted, only "dabbling in pre-history". It was regrettable that *Fortnight* magazine, which has an excellent track record for genuinely authoritative articles, gave up valuable space to this seriously flawed diatribe.

A Wasted Opportunity

My experiences in cross-community work throughout the present 'troubles' have convinced me that the media constantly play a negative role in events, showing little imagination or sense of responsibility. Hence, when I was approached by BBC Radio Ulster to take part in a programme about the Cruthin (*The Cruthin–A Common Culture?*[29]) I refused, as did Ian Adamson. However, the producer, Louis Edmondson, was persistent, and mainly because we found him a very likeable person we relented and agreed to take part – on certain conditions. My primary hesitation stemmed from a suspicion that the media were more interested in the *controversy* surrounding the Cruthin, rather than any real concern with exploring our belief in the shared heritage of the Ulster people. The producer assured us that the 'controversy' would *not* be his primary concern, though he would obviously be making mention of it, as we had to admit that our work *had* stirred up controversy. He further assured us that the programme would be 'balanced'. I finally insisted that I hear a recording of the programme *before* it went out – as much because there had been so much rubbish spouted (both from political and academic sources) about what we had *never* said – otherwise my contribution was to be deleted.

Not to our great surprise, no-one ever appeared with the promised recording, and the commitments given about maintaining a 'balance' and minimising the 'controversy', as far as we were concerned were not kept. I wrote to the producer with my analysis of his programme. Of its 55 minutes duration, academic critics of 'Cruthinism' were allocated 34.7% of this time; Young Unionists with their own 'interpretations', 8.0%; interludes of music and readings, 36.2%; a neutral archaeologist, 2.1%; and Adamson and myself, 16.5%. The portion given over to the academic critics and the Unionist 'interpreters' was *primarily* concerned with the 'controversy' – a full 42.7% of the programme, which, considering the 36.2% of musical interludes, did not leave much time for anything else.

Nor did we see much evidence of 'balance'. The Unionist 'interpreters' and the academic critics were permitted to air their positions before Adamson was brought in (somewhat surprising, given that he was the main exponent of 'Cruthinism'); indeed, he did not make an appearance until the 22nd minute, almost half way through the programme! Up until then he had not even been mentioned – the academics had addressed their criticisms to what "Unionists are saying", what "Unionists are trying to project..." or lamenting that "Unionists [are] using and abusing history...", ample proof of the fixation, by the academics and the producer, with the 'controversy'. Then, to end the programme, "the final word", rather than being given to Adamson (as might have been expected, considering his primary role in the subject) was deferentially left to his most bitter academic critic. All in all, hardly what I would define as 'balance'.

In truth, the broken promises did not unduly annoy us – after all, we should have known better. Far more disappointing was that an opportunity to present a properly researched programme – with an academic critique *included* – which went *beyond* the fixation with any 'controversy', and created greater awareness among the public about this aspect of our *shared* heritage, was completely wasted.

Columbanus – A Suitable Case for Treatment?
On the same radio programme, Richard Warner, as one of the academic critics, categorically stated that the Cruthin were "rather minor and they are rather unimportant and they made very little influence on Irish power or politics".[29] Now, apart from giving the impression that Warner viewed the Cruthin with some distaste – why else would he endeavour to squeeze *three* separate derogatory comments ("rather minor", "rather unimportant", "very little influence") into *one* short sentence? – the statement was also remarkably inaccurate. For even if

we were to consider *just one* of the Cruthin – the abbot Comgall – Warner's assertion appears quite ludicrous.

I have already made mention of Comgall and his monastic foundation at Bangor, "which has given the largest number of names to Irish religious history – Columbanus, Gall, Moluag, Maelrubha, Dungal, Malachy, to name but a few."[40] I also pointed out that one of Comgall's disciples, Columbanus, who departed from Bangor in 595, left an indelible mark on the history of Europe. Pope Pius XI wrote: "The more light that is shed by scholars in the period known as the Middle Ages the clearer it becomes that it was thanks to the initiative and labours of Columbanus that the rebirth of Christian virtue and civilisation over a great part of Gaul, Germany and Italy took place."[8(B)] The French poet Leon Cathlin concluded: "He is, with Charlemagne, the greatest figure of our Early Middle Ages."

All this had stemmed directly from the energies of the abbot Comgall, a representative of the Cruthin, who are now apparently regarded by a 'professional' scholar as "rather minor and... rather unimportant and they made very little influence on Irish power or politics"!

Even if the Cruthin had thrown up no major historical personages such as St Comgall or Congal Cláen, academics, including those antagonistic to Adamson, now accept that the Cruthin formed "the bulk of the population"[33] of Ulster following its contraction under the pressure of Uí Néill territorial expansion. To assert that the bulk of the population – the ordinary people – are "rather minor" in their country's history is pure elitism. Furthermore, Warner's 'interpretation' of the Cruthin as being 'minor and unimportant' highlights once again that his claim that it is "the job of people like me to know when... historical interpretation is likely to be correct or incorrect"[51] is somewhat suspect.

To highlight the difficulties we have repeatedly faced when trying to promote a cross-community awareness of our shared heritage, I will stay for a moment with the story of Columbanus, for he seemed an ideal subject for a cross-community initiative, and in early 1990 a group was formed to design a suitable project.

The group decided that this project (which had the enthusiastic support of Cardinal Tomás Ó Fiaich, who had written a biography of Columbanus) should have three components: (i) a video would be made by Farset Community Project detailing the significance of Columbanus; (ii) an essay competition in the schools would select a group of teenagers – from both traditions – who would spend part of their summer vacation travelling across Europe, following in the 'footsteps of Columbanus'; and (iii) I would write a book on the wider story of Ireland's 'religious' heritage – exploring not only the story of Columbanus and the history of the early church, but the dolmen-builders, the Elder Faiths, and even the fascinating survival today, alongside Christian beliefs, of pagan superstitions, such as rural respect for 'fairy thorns'. The book was to be aimed at a 'popular' audience and would be extensively illustrated.

The book proposal was submitted to the Cultural Traditions Group of the Community Relations Council for financial assistance. We felt confident such assistance would be forthcoming, for here was a project which: (i) was cross-community in composition; (ii) was dealing with an aspect of Ulster's heritage which belonged to the whole community; and (iii) was trying to direct our usually parochial concerns *outwards*, by involving a European dimension – the young people's trip was scheduled for 1992, a significant year for the European Community. Yet, to the dismay of project members, the application was turned down! I wrote to the Cultural Traditions Group seeking an explanation, and was told: "In relation to 'The Steps of Columbanus', the Publications Group decided that it was not the kind of publication that they wish to support." [41]

Although there were other problems, from this moment on our hopes for the project began to unravel, and although a rough pilot video was made,[42] the idea had to be shelved, another wasted opportunity which had floundered as much because of a lack of vision from those in a position to assist.

[Perhaps no-one is interested in helping the people of Ulster look outwards – the academic volume referred to earlier[28] made no mention of either Comgall or Columbanus, let alone their contribution to European history.]

"He *used* to be a good scholar..."

I remarked that the Columbanus Project had the support of Cardinal Tomás Ó Fiaich. In fact, he had been a supporter of our work for some time. In 1979 he wrote to Adamson about *The Cruthin*, saying: "There is not all that much I would be inclined to disagree with in it and even in cases where I might not see eye to eye with you I think it is more a matter of different interpretations – equally justifiable – of the same material." [43]

Unlike many academics and reviewers, Cardinal Ó Fiaich had no difficulty seeing the cross-community purpose behind our work, and wrote, for the second edition of Adamson's *Bangor: Light of the World*: "I deem it a high honour to be invited to write this foreword to it... I hope that [this] new edition will have a wide circulation... It provides that most unusual thing at the present time – a book about the religious history of Ulster, of which both Protestant and Catholic, both Nationalist and Unionist, can be equally proud." [8(B)]

Cardinal Ó Fiaich was not only extremely likeable as a person, but, in contrast to many of our academics and reviewers, was eager to engage in constructive dialogue on all aspects of our history. He had taken part in a series of BBC Radio Ulster lectures, his own contribution, 'The Celts', being printed in *The Irish News*. [44] However, in his lecture he said: "The Picts in the north and other Pre-Celtic peoples left few traces. Apart from the surviving field monuments their legacy is found only in museums." While I thought his lecture excellent, I felt I had to take issue with him over the veracity of that comment, and *The Irish News* published my response,[45] (see Appendix) in which I suggested that the pre-Celtic population and their legacy, rather than leaving few traces, remained as a vibrant part of the Irish heritage. While many of our academics might have disdainfully ignored such criticism, Tomás Ó Fiaich was of a different calibre, and when we next met told me I had been right to take him to task. When the lecture series eventually reappeared as a book, he had even amended that passage to read: "The Picts in the north and other pre-Celtic peoples were overthrown. No doubt they still formed a strong element in the population but they were assimilated in language and culture." [46]

His close interest in our endeavours was ample proof that it *is* possible for people from different backgrounds to explore our history in a manner which, while not losing anything to objectivity or accuracy, endeavours to encompass *all* the traditions and peoples who have contributed to this island's historical legacy. Indeed, who knows where his collaboration with us might have led if it had not been ended by his untimely death at Lourdes.

Or am I being naive – perhaps any collaboration would have been sabotaged by our academic elite? A few years before the Cardinal's death, Ian Adamson, while leaving the BBC studios after a radio debate, mentioned to the prominent academic who had been his adversary that scholars like Tomás Ó Fiaich (who had been Professor of History at St Patrick's College, Maynooth) supported his work. "Cardinal Ó Fiaich?" replied the academic, "He *used* to be a good scholar."

The Cardinal had obviously been associating with the 'wrong' type of people.

Interpretations at the Extremes
It has to be admitted that the use (and misuse) of the work of Adamson and myself by sections of the Protestant community has contributed greatly to the unease with which 'Cruthinism' has been viewed.

The way some Loyalists have 'interpreted' the story of the Cruthin undoubtedly has its roots in the trauma experienced by the Protestant community over the past quarter century, with former certainties eroded and old loyalties rebuffed. To the feeling of being 'under siege' from Catholic/Gaelic/Irish nationalism has been added the fear of an eventual betrayal by Britain. To counter this twin-edged threat, 'Cruthinism' was seized upon by some Loyalists as a "we were here first" counterbalance to the rampant Republican assault, and as a possible alternative 'identity' to replace any severance of the link with Britain.

On top of this need for a substitute identity was often added blatant misinterpretation. Some within the Loyalist community seemed to imagine that, by some miracle, the present Protestant population were all direct descendents of the Cruthin, and likewise the Catholic community were all direct descendents of the Gaels. In this way, no doubt, ancient battles could now be fought against present enemies.

Patient work is going on to rectify such misinterpretations and the hope is that our efforts will eventually set matters straight. Indeed, it must be said that many individuals within the Protestant community, including some considered 'hard-line', have shown a genuine willingness to embrace the cross-community basis of 'Cruthinism', and, despite the constant efforts by academia to thwart our efforts, we feel confident in the eventual outcome.

The Irish Nationalist/Republican interpretation is also indicative of their community's identity needs and 'certainties'. The suggestion that the Irish may not be pure Celts after all, and that the northern Protestants have roots in Ireland long predating the Plantation, has not been that warmly received by many staunch Nationalists. Indeed, they have been more than willing to collude with the misinterpretations of 'Cruthinism' purveyed by extreme Loyalists. In that way it can be denigrated more readily, and any perceived threat neutralised.

When I completed the first draft of *Ulster–The Hidden History* in 1986, I gave copies to individuals in both communities, requesting feedback as to how my theme of a *shared* history was viewed. My discussions with Republicans revealed that, even when their suspicions as to the 'purpose' behind such a history were allayed, any talk of a 'shared history' was still something of a distraction, and played little part in the Republican consciousness. The Republican movement already had its 'history' and considered it quite adequate. Indeed, the only 'shared history' Republicans felt necessary was one which encouraged the Protestant community to join with them in a United Ireland.

The current Republican assessment of 'Cruthinism' seemingly adjudges it to be either a cry from the heart for Protestants to rediscover their Irish identity or a right-wing Loyalist counterbalance to Irish Nationalism. Within this dichotomy Republicans ignore the more obvious interpretation – that 'Cruthinism' is just what we have always stressed: an aspect of our history which reveals not only what the two Northern communities hold in common, but what the people of our two islands hold in common. It is obvious that such an interpretation of our ancient history makes uncomfortable reading for many, Loyalists *and* Republicans.

Ironically, if 'Cruthinism' was allowed to develop without political manipulation or academic hindrance, *both* communities could gain from it, without it threatening any deeply-held beliefs. Republicans could strengthen *their* case by convincing the Protestant community of their obvious 'Irishness', while Loyalists could help convince their Catholic fellow-countrymen that *they too* have ancient links with mainland Britain. Eventually, both traditions might come to see themselves as complementary rather than as antagonistic, and new social and political arrangements might be more easily developed which could give tangible structure to this new understanding.

The Wheel Comes Full Circle
Brian Lambkin hinted at a change in academic perception: "What is encouraging is that Adamson, on the evidence of his latest book, *The Ulster People*, is in touch

with recent scholarship and sees himself less as an outsider." [22] But we would contend that Adamson has never been *out* of touch with scholarship, it is certain sections within academia who have been out of touch, and are only now being forced to change tack. Let us assess the current situation:

Books on Ulster's history rarely appear now without mention of the Cruthin. Admittedly some of the authors rarely lose an opportunity to take a swipe at Adamson, but the Cruthin are no longer denied – an ancient people have finally 'come of age'. The debate now centres on *who* they actually were, *not* on whether they ever existed other than in Adamson's fertile imagination. The fact that they once formed the majority population in parts of Ulster is granted, even by academics with a distaste for 'Cruthinism'. Books now make mention of the Battle of Moira and its main protagonist, the Cruthin over-king of Ulster, Congal Cláen. Even the abbot Comgall and the importance of his monastic foundation at Bangor to European history must surely make a reappearance – notwithstanding a conspicuous absence in the first major academic history of Ulster published since the 1950s.

The probability that the Irish people are of predominantly pre-Celtic stock is also firmly on the agenda. Adamson certainly cannot claim credit for this – a sustained assault on the notion of a pure Celtic race has been underway for some time – yet 'Cruthinism' has helped force the issue to the surface among our academics. Jonathan Bardon, in his *A History of Ulster*, acknowledged the new reality: "Scholars are coming increasingly to the realisation that Celtic civilisation was not the creation of a separate race but a language and a way of life spread from one people to another. Archaeological enquiry does not show evidence of formidable invasion." [47]

A pre-Celtic cultural and genetic relationship between the peoples of Ireland and Scotland is now accepted as a strong probability – even if not attributed to the Cruthin and Picts. Though not all academics are averse to such a suggestion. In the latest edition of the *Oxford Illustrated History of Ireland*, Donnchadh Ó Corráin, in his chapter on 'Prehistoric and Early Christian Ireland', remarks:

> What is interesting, too, is the mixed racial and linguistic background of the rulers of Ireland – Britain and Ireland share languages, dominant aristocracies, and whole local populations such as the Cruithin of Ireland and Scotland (where they are known to Latin writers as Picti). [48]

Will Ó Corráin be pilloried as was Adamson – after all he has committed two cardinal sins: he has not only dared to accord a prominent place to a people who are supposedly "rather minor and rather unimportant", but has linked them with the Picts of Scotland. Or will our academics now bow to the inevitable? Has the wheel finally begun to turn full circle?

Cross-Community Hope
Adamson, in the preface to *The Cruthin* made his appeal to both communities quite explicit: "It is my purpose... to give [the people] back the history which

has been denied them for so long, for they are the Ancient Kindred of Ireland as well as Britain. In so doing I hope that their origins will provide for them a basis of common identity rather than the cause of that running sore which is 'The War in Ireland'." [8(A)]

Yet academics like H J Morgan endeavour to assert that Adamson's "view of Ulster history" is "exclusivist and supremacist" [21], and journalists allege that his work is "vaguely reminiscent of the Blut and Erde ideology of German nationalism which ended in the gas chambers." [25] Many others certainly did not see it that way, including scholars such as Cardinal Tomás Ó Fiaich and Professor René Fréchet (founder of the Institute of Irish Studies at the Sorbonne, who died in 1993 before his translation of *The Ulster People* was completed). How can such a disparity of views exist? My belief is that such allegations bear little relation to what Adamson is *really* saying but have their origin in academia's own 'hidden agenda', and the deferential acceptance accorded academic opinions within the media.

However, the surest way to assess the veracity of such allegations – and reflect on the purpose being served by them – is for readers to judge for themselves. We are confident that those who read *The Ulster People* will concur with the view expressed in it that this history is, if anything, an attack on 'exclusivist' views:

> In many ways a cultural battle is now on, in which interpretations of history are right to the forefront. It is a battle in which narrow and exclusive interpretations, which served to consolidate each community's supposed hegemony of righteousness, are under attack from a much broader and inclusive interpretation of *all* the facets which go to make up our identity. A positive outcome of this battle might just help to drag the Ulster people away from their obsessions with distorted history and the divisive attitudes of the past. [8(E)]

Not content with his 'supremacist' allegation, Morgan also stated that "what must be realised is that there are no prior or exclusive claims; that we are a mixed race today as in the past," as if no-one else has 'realised' this, least of all Adamson. Yet Adamson has been saying it all along:

> In the South the time had come, as Bob Quinn suggested, when the Irish people "must develop the confidence to dismantle the unitary myth that has served its honourable purpose and replace it with the diverse richness that lies within." [49] In Northern Ireland, a dislike of anything 'Irish', and a subservience to 'English' history within the schools, had left the Protestant community there not only unaware of most aspects of Irish history, but, more, significantly, without any real understanding of the history of their own province. Yet Ulster's historical and cultural heritage was not only extremely rich and varied, but contained within it the proof of the common identity of the Northerners. Slowly, as contemporary flawed history was called into question and a new awareness emerged, the facts of their history, rather than dividing them, offered the hope of uniting the Ulster people at last. [8(E)]

Sources

1. Peter C Woodman, *The Mesolithic in Ireland*, British Arachaeological Report 58, 1978.
2. Séan P O Ríordáin, *Antiquities of the Irish Countryside*, Methuen, 1973.
3. Peter Woodman, 'Prehistoric Settlers', *The People of Ireland*, edited by Patrick Loughrey, Appletree Press/BBC, Belfast, 1988.
4. J P Mallory, 'The Origins of the Irish', *The Journal of Irish Archaeology*, II, 1984.
5. Eoin MacNeill, section on 'History' in *Saorstát Eireann Official Handbook*, Dublin, 1932.
6. W A Hanna, 'More annals of Ulster', *Fortnight*, January 1994.
7. Francis J Byrne, 'Early Irish Society', in *The Course of Irish History*, ed. by Moody and Martin, Mercier Press, 1984.
8. Ian Adamson: (A) *The Cruthin* (1974); (B) *Bangor–Light of the World* (1979); (C) *The Battle of Moira* (1980); (D) *The Identity of Ulster* (1982); (E) *The Ulster People* (1991), Pretani Press, Belfast.
9. T F O'Rahilly, *Early Irish History and Mythology*, Dublin Institute for Advanced Studies, 1984.
10. Thomas L Markey, 'The Language of Stonehenge', *L.S.A.*, University of Michigan, 1988.
11. Liam de Paor, 'The People of Ireland', in *The People of Ireland*, edited by Patrick Loughrey, Appletree Press/BC, Belfast, 1988.
12. *Annals of Ulster*, edited with a translation and notes, by William M Hennessy, HMSO, Dublin, 1887.
13. *The Battle of Moira*, Samuel Ferguson's 'Congal', edited by Ian Adamson, Pretani Press, Belfast, 1980.
14. Francis J Byrne, *Irish Kings and High Kings*, Batsford, London, 1973.
15. *The Illustrated Road Book of Ireland*, The Automobile Association, 1970.
16. Adamnani, *Vita S. Columbae*, edited from Dr Reeves' text with an introduction by J T Fowler, Oxford, 1894.
17. Michael Hall, *Ulster's Scottish Connection*, 'Island Pamphlets: 3', Island Publications, 1993.
18. Michael Hall, *Ulster's Shared Heritage*, 'Island Pamphlets: 6', Island Publications, 1993.
19. Michael Hall, *Ulster: The Hidden History*, Pretani Press, Belfast, 1986 & 1989.
20. Peter Carr, review of 'The Cruthin' (Adamson) and 'Ulster: the Hidden History' (Hall), *Linen Hall Review*, Spring 1987.
21. H J Morgan, 'Deceptions of demons', *Fortnight*, September 1993.
22. B K Lambkin, 'Navan Fort and the Arrival of "Cultural Heritage" ', *Emania*, no. 11, 1993.
23. James Ferris, review of 'The Red Hand' (Bruce), *Linen Hall Review*, Winter 1992.
24. Hiram Morgan, 'Milesians, Ulstermen and Fenians', *Linen Hall Review*, December 1991.
25. John Hunter, 'Now, councillor, yer talkin' sense', *The Irish News*, 28.01.94.
26. Bill Rolston, *Politics and Painting: Murals and Conflict in Northern Ireland*, Associated University Presses, 1991.

27. 'Ireland: History', W K Sullivan & Richard Bagwell, *Encyclopaedia Britannica*, ninth edition, 1876–1886.

28. *Ulster: An Illustrated History*, edited by Ciaran Brady, Mary O'Dowd and Brian Walker, Batsford, London, 1989.

29. *The Cruthin–A Common Culture?* BBC Radio Ulster, 12.07.89.

30. Peter Carr, review of 'The Archaeology of Ulster' (Mallory and McNeill), *Linen Hall Review*, Summer 1993.

31. Oonagh Warke, 'Red hand me down', *Books Ireland*, March 1993.

32. P.B., *New Ulster*, The Journal of the Ulster Society, March 1987.

33. Charles Doherty, 'Ulster before the Normans: ancient myth and early history', *Ulster: An Illustrated History*, Batsford, London, 1989.

34. Richard B Warner, 'Cultural Intrusions in the Early Iron Age: Some Notes', *Emania*, Bulletin of the Navan Research Group, no. 9, 1991.

35. J P Mallory & T E McNeill, *The Archaeology of Ulster from Colonisation to Plantation*, The Institute of Irish Studies, Queen's University of Belfast, 1991.

36. *Belfast Telegraph*, 22.01.92

37. Aidan Walsh, 'Excavating the Black Pig's Dyke', *Emania*, No. 3, Autumn 1987.

38. Eoin MacNeill, *Phases of Irish History*, Gill & Son, Dublin, 1919.

39. R A S Macalister, *Ireland in Pre-Celtic Times*, Mannsell & Roberts, 1921.

40. Mary Ryan D'Arcy, *The Saints of Ireland*, The Irish American Cultural Institute, Minnesota, 1974.

41. *Letter* to author from Maurna Crozier, Cultural Traditions Group, 30.10.90.

42. Copies may be borrowed from Farset Community Project, 638 Springfield Road, Belfast.

43. *Letter* from Tomás Ó Fiaich to Ian Adamson, 02.02.79.

44. Cardinal Tomás Ó Fiaich, 'The Celts', *The Irish News*, 01.12.86.

45. Michael Hall, 'Time to credit pre-Celts for making of the Irish', *The Irish News*, 05.01.87.

46. Tomás Ó Fiaich, 'The Celts: 1', *The People of Ireland*, edited by Patrick Loughrey, Appletree Press/BBC, Belfast, 1988.

47. Jonathan Bardon, *A History of Ulster*, The Blackstaff Press, Belfast, 1992.

48. Donnchadh Ó Corráin, 'Prehistoric and Early Christian Ireland', *The Oxford Illustrated History of Ireland*, edited by R F Foster, Oxford University Press, 1993.

49. Bob Quinn, *Atlantean*, Quartet Books, London, 1986.

Appendix

'Time to credit pre-Celts for making of the Irish'

(article appearing in *The Irish News*, 05.01.87)

Cardinal Tomás Ó Fiaich's recent article 'The Celts' in the *Irish News* was fascinating and authoritative. [1] However, while his celebration of Ireland's Celtic heritage was perfectly legitimate, I feel it was misleading in its exclusiveness. I refer specifically to his statements: "The Picts in the north and other Pre-Celtic peoples left few traces. Apart from the surviving field monuments, their legacy is found only in museums."

It seems to me that rather than having been relegated to the dusty shelves of museums, the 'legacy' of Ireland's pre-Celtic inhabitants is very much alive, not only because of its ancestral importance to the make-up of the unique Irish personality, but because it is still evident in our folk ways, and deep relationship with the land.

Mainly because the inhabitants of this island adopted the Gaelic language there has been the erroneous inference in many quarters that the Irish people are a purely Celtic race. Yet no-one would dare claim that we have become an 'English' race, just because we have now adopted the English language.

As Cardinal Ó Fiaich pointed out, it is futile to try and speculate as to the numbers of Celts who arrived here, but at least we can suggest their *relative* size in comparison to the population they found already established.

In his summation of the deliberations of a gathering of highly eminent academics in 1984, J P Mallory stated that it was more than probable that the Celtic immigrations into Ireland "were carried out by populations numerically far inferior to the native population(s)." [2]

The Celts obviously had a military prowess and capability disproportionate to their small numbers, that allowed them to gain a commanding superiority (in much the same way that a handful of Englishmen were able to dominate the whole Indian subcontinent), but they did not evict the indigenous people.

As Eoin MacNeill wrote: "The notion that the migratory conquests of antiquity resulted in the displacement of one population by another is one of the favourite illusions of popular history." [3]

Furthermore, T W Rolleston had suggested that because of their warlike proclivities, the Celtic warrior chiefs "perished in far greater proportion than the earlier populations whom they had themselves subjugated." [4] I would suspect, however, that these warrior chiefs, like all military castes or ruling establishments, were just as content to let the ordinary people perish as cannon fodder in the endless battles on their behalf.

If we accept that the Celts were only a small minority in Ireland, then, in terms of our actual ancestry, we obviously owe more to the pre-Celtic inhabitants.

As Estyn Evans suggested: "If it were possible to sort out the genes of the Irish people, I would hazard a guess that those coming from English settlers would exceed those deriving from 'the Celts', and that those coming from older stocks would constitute the largest proportion." [5]

So, having highlighted the likely numerical inferiority of the Celts who reached

29

Ireland, we are left seeing our primary heritage as due, not to a genetic basis after all, but to aspects of their culture.

Cardinal Ó Fiaich listed many of those aspects most commonly believed to derive from the Celts, including "our most outstanding native saints and missionaries, the majority language until the Famine, a splendid native music and one of the richest folklores in the world." But let us look a little closer at these.

The Irish language has been described by scholars as "bizarre" in its composite make-up, and Professor David Green said: "Irish is a language made in Ireland; it is neither Indo-European nor Celtic, Pictish or Hamitic, but simply the linguistic expression of the Irish people." [6]

Not all of the greatest saints and missionaries were Celts. At St Comgall's great monastery of Bangor, from where Columbanus and Gall set out on their great missions to Europe, Francis Byrne points out that "Comgall and the early abbots had been Cruthin." [7]

The *Cruthin*, Byrne points out elsewhere, were part of "the earlier, non-Indo-European population [who] survived under the Celtic overlordship." [8] Ian Adamson has elaborated further on the legacy we owe to the Cruthin people.

Many academics see most Irish folk mores as basically pre-Celtic, and much of our rich assortment of unique folk customs, superstitions, and folk lore probably dates back to a pre-Celtic past. Such folk memories and beliefs have persisted even to this day with remarkable force, having proved impervious to the religions of the Celts and the Christians and even to the new religion of materialism.

As Evans mused in *Irish heritage*: "A venerable thorn, pink-flowering, stands under my window as I write and casts its shadow into the Senate Room of the University. But no one will remove it or even lop its branches, and the story goes that when the buildings were being erected the plans had to be changed in order that the thorn should not be interfered with. If a lone tree surrounded by half a dozen scientific departments has claimed such respect it can be imagined in what awe the country thorns are held!" [9]

Our traditional music, too, is felt by some to have very deep roots in our ancient past.

All the new groups that set foot in Ireland during the last two millenia, while obviously engendering some local adaption, were still to a large extent absorbed into Irish life and personality. The Vikings and the Anglo-Normans stand out most in the popular imagination. But so too do the descendants of the 17th century Planters, for despite all their vociferous claims to 'true Britishness' they are more 'Irish', albeit of a distinctly Northern variety, than they ever were 'British'. And if they refuse to see that, at least the mainland British themselves are not deluded.

Yet somehow the Celts, despite being "numerically far inferior" to the indigenous inhabitants, are frequently said to have 'absorbed' or 'assimilated' the majority population. Why were the Celts the exception then? Is it just the legacy of 'their' language? Or does it just reflect the way the Irish romantically like to see it?

Is it not more probable that the already established peoples in many ways absorbed the Celts, or at least were an equal partner in the cross-fertilisation of ideas and customs.

Evans asked: "Did the Celts conquer Ireland, or did Ireland conquer the Celts?" He painted an alternative scenario when he suggested that there had been "a reluctance in Ireland to see Gaelic society as evolving from the adjustment of a conquering aristocracy to a novel and difficult environment occupied by an obstinate and strongly conservative native population. In many parts of the country, especially among the hills, these would probably have far outnumbered the newcomers. The popular conception of the Gael as a noble creature – every Irishman's ancestor – living in splendid isolation relieved by grand periodic assemblies seems to be the joint product of the national revival and of the Romantic movement." [5]

The places the Celts selected as power bases had also been revered by the indigenous people from Neolithic times. Were the Celts forced to incorporate, or bow down to, local sensitivities, just as the later Christian church, unable to remove many folk customs, had to incorporate them into Christian practice, and make Holy Days of pagan festivities?

I am not trying here to deny a vital, invigorating and innovative role to the Celts and their imagination, I merely feel we should recognise that their input was only one part of a 'shared' heritage, shared with the needs, customs, creativities and capabilities of the masses of the long-established pre-Celtic people. The Celts in their great sagas talk derisively of the subject peoples, but we must not fall into the same trap.

In many ways, the whole issue is about how we look at history. Is history made by a few 'great' men, politicians or armies, or is it made by the constant but hidden efforts of ordinary people? Did Belfast's renowned image of industriousness belong solely to the managerial establishment, or did it not really belong to the generations of families who provided the manpower from among the huddled rows of working-class housing?

This question of to whom belongs the real legacy of our history – to the rulers or the people – led R A S Macalister to make the following speculation: "Christianity ever brings its message of freedom to the serf: through its influence, the enslaved aboriginal folk, the Picts, were at least partially relieved from the burden of oppression that had crushed them down to the dust. Is it a mere coincidence that this emancipation is synchronous with the sudden manifestation of art? Have the Celts been usurping a glory which is not theirs? Are the Ardagh Cup and the Gospel of Kells the thanksofferings of a people long enslaved, and come to their own once again?" [10]

I contend that rather than dismiss our pre-Celtic heritage as 'lost' or only to be found in museums, a new reassessment must be made. Such a new awareness should only serve to highlight just how ancient and multifaceted our rich and unique heritage really is, and strengthen the cultural pride that belongs to all the Irish people, a people reckoned to be one of the longest settled populations of western Europe.

Michael Hall

1   Tomás Ó Fiaich, 'The Celts', *The Irish News*, 01.12.86.
2   J P Mallory, 'The Origins of the Irish', *The Journal of Irish Archaeology*, II, 1984.
3   Eoin MacNeill, *Phases of Irish History*, Gill and Son, 1919.
4   T W Rolleston, *Myths and Legends of the Celtic Race*, Constable, London, 1985.
5   Estyn Evans, *The Personality of Ireland*, Blackstaff Press, Belfast, 1981.
6   David Green, *The Irish Language*, Dublin, 1966.
7   Francis Byrne, *Irish Kings and High Kings*, Batsford, 1973.
8   Francis Byrne, 'Early Irish Society', *The Course of Irish History*, The Mercier Press, 1984.
9   Estyn Evans, *Irish Heritage*, Dundalgan Press, 1942.
10 R A S Macalister, *Ancient Ireland*, Methuen, 1935.

Island Pamphlets

1. ## LIFE AT THE INTERFACE

   Report of a Conference held on 8.10.92 and attended by community groups from the Shankill, Falls and Springfield Roads in Belfast.

2. ## SACRIFICE ON THE SOMME

   Michael Hall

   A description of the Battle of the Somme (and subsequent battles), 1916, focusing on the 'cross-community' nature of the sacrifice in Ulster lives. Includes testimony from veterans.

3. ## ULSTER'S SCOTTISH CONNECTION

   Michael Hall

   An exploration of the unique links between Ulster and Scotland, proving that the historical and cultural heritage of the peoples on either side of the North Channel – and also the divided people of Ulster themselves – is very much a shared one.

4. ## IDLE HOURS

   Robert Atkinson and Robert Atkinson jnr.

   Belfast working-class poetry.

5. ## EXPECTING THE FUTURE

   Michael Hall

   A community play intended as a reading script for young people, to encourage discussion on the emotional effects of Northern Ireland's violence upon individuals and communities.

6. ## ULSTER'S SHARED HERITAGE

   Michael Hall

   An exploration of the rich, unique and *shared* historical and cultural inheritance of the Ulster people.

Priced £1.50 each

Available from bookshops or direct from the publisher:

Island Publications, 132 Serpentine Road, Newtownabbey, Co Antrim BT36 7JQ